God
(Still)
Whispers

God (Still) Whispers

ENCOURAGEMENT THROUGH BREAST CANCER WITH GOD'S HELP

Wendi Kelley

Cover Design: Leslie Jones
Cover Artwork: Patrick Folker

ISBN: **979-8-9861237-0-7**

This book is dedicated to God.
Without His unending love, mercy, grace,
and healing favor I would not be
able to share my story in hopes
to help others.

TABLE OF CONTENTS

Introduction

About the Author

Let us Run
the race that is set before us,
Looking to Jesus
the founder and perfecter of
our faith.

Hebrews 12:1b-2a ESV

INTRODUCTION

While this book was difficult to write, I also felt it was also very important and exciting. This, my friend, is a story about how God is *still* alive and active in our lives, and I cannot wait to share it with you!

As I began to work on this project, I was watching a series about the life of Jesus. In one particular scene, He was speaking to a gathering of people and using a parable about fishermen. He explained that the parables He told would mean something to some of the people, but not to everyone. I am approaching this book in that way. I am prayerful that He will use what I present as a means to reach different people, in various ways, but always in a way that glorifies Him.

This story is about encouragement for breast cancer patients and their families. While each patient's story and experience is different, I hope this will give you some insight about what you can expect as a patient. And if your loved one is battling breast cancer, I offer some ways you can help, because I know you feel helpless much of the time.

I have been aware of what I refer to as "God whispers" for a long time. They can be little coincidences or "signs" that I recognize as God letting me know He is with me. (Honestly, that's another book in itself, because there have been so many of these signs!) His whispers also come to me like a little voice in the back of my head. Usually it is very faint, but occasionally it is quite loud, and there is no denying Who it is. God-whispers became a focus of mine about five or six years ago. I posted something on social media about it a few years back, and that laid the groundwork for this project to some degree.

One of the purposes of this book is to help you, one sister to another sister or brother. Once you come out on the other side of it all, I hope you will allow God to work through you to guide, support, and comfort others.

I wrote this as if you and I have been friends for a long time. I imagine we are sitting on my couch, drinking coffee, and having a conversation. I said at the beginning of my breast cancer journey that if my experience could help one person, just *one* person, then it would be worth it. I was thinking small-scale, such as helping someone I know, or a friend of a friend, who had been diagnosed. And I was blessed to be able to do that. But God had other ideas. He was thinking larger scale.

While my perspective on navigating through the breast cancer process is an important part of what I want to share, it's not the most important part. I believe the greater significance lies in my being able to share with you that God is with you. He wants you to lean on Him as you are going through the progression of diagnosis, treatment plan, treatment, and recovery. I also hope to give you some things to think about and a few suggestions of how to make this difficult time in your life and the life of your loved one a little easier.

You're probably familiar with the story in 1 Kings 19, where God communicates with Elijah. Elijah had shown God's power on Mount Carmel against the idol of Baal. As a result, Jezebel, King Ahab's wife, wanted to have him killed. Elijah fled into the desert, and an angel appeared to him several times, providing food. Eventually, Elijah reached Mount Horeb and it was there that God told Elijah, in verses 11–12 (ESV):

> *"Go out and stand on the mount before the Lord." And behold, the Lord passed by, and a great and strong wind tore the mountains and broke in*
> *pieces the rocks before the Lord, but the Lord*
> *was not in the wind. And after the wind an earthquake, but the Lord was not in the*
> *earthquake. And after the earthquake, a fire,*
> *but the Lord was not in the fire. And after the*
> *fire, the sound of a low whisper."*

The prophet had anticipated God would speak in shock-and-awe — in the howling wind, the earthquake, or the fire. But He didn't. Instead God spoke in a still, small voice. A whisper.

He hushed the storm
to a gentle whisper
So that the waves of the sea
were still.

Psalm 107:29 AMP

CHAPTER 1

MY STORY- DIAGNOSIS AND BEYOND

I went in for my annual mammogram on August 2, 2018. Unfortunately, I forgot to have my screening done in 2017, because I had just started a new position at work. There was so much going on at that time that it slipped my mind. I think this was the first time I had ever missed an appointment since I started having mammograms. I got a phone call from the doctor's office and the voice on the other end said that there was something a little off. She wanted me to come in for a follow-up appointment. I went in on August 14 and had another mammogram as well as an ultrasound. A few days later, I received another call and was told that there was an area they were concerned about, and I was referred to a surgeon. I met with the surgeon on August 21 for a biopsy and a consult. Honestly, at this point I knew in my heart what the result of the biopsy was going to show.

I went back a week later, on Monday, August 27, to learn what the biopsy determined. The surgeon confirmed it; I had breast cancer. They showed me where it was located, and I could feel it. It felt like a small, hard pea. Had I been doing monthly self-examinations like we've all been instructed to do, I may have found it sooner. I encourage anyone reading this to perform their self-exams on a monthly basis. The surgeon asked me what I wanted to do.

That was a shocker. I thought to myself, *'What do you mean, what do I want to do? I have no idea what is going on, what I'm supposed to think, how I am supposed to react, what I'm supposed to say…. What do you mean, what do I want to do??? YOU are the professional for crying out loud! Aren't YOU the one who is supposed to tell ME what I need to do??? I've never had breast cancer before. This is my first rodeo. Surely you have worked with breast cancer patients before. What did THEY do? Because I DON'T KNOW WHAT I WANT TO DO!'*

But all I could say was, "I don't know." In truth, I knew the one thing I wanted to do, and desperately needed to do, was to pray. But I wasn't even sure what to pray for. And that's what I told God. I told Him that I wanted to pray but wasn't even sure what to say and what to ask for. Then He told me: guidance and clarity. I heard His whisper telling me

I needed to pray for guidance and clarity, and that's exactly what I did. The surgeon scheduled me for an MRI the next day, August 28. I was given some informational brochures and pamphlets that explained what breast cancer is, surgery and treatment options, and what I could expect in the upcoming weeks and months. I was to go back to see her on August 30 for the results of the MRI and tell her what I wanted to do.

On Wednesday, August 29, we made the announcement at church that I had been diagnosed with breast cancer and that I was asking for prayers from the church. I was honored with a beautiful prayer where God was asked to watch over me during the next few days and months. The congregation was dismissed to go to Bible class and several folks came over and gave me the best hugs and told me that they would continue to pray for me. Then Ms. Medrith Anschultz came to see me.

I must now pause my story and give you a little bit of background on Ms. Med. She is one of the matriarchs of our church. She and her husband, Lannas, are some of the best people you will ever meet. With the exception of my parents, they are the most kind, generous, loving, and Godly examples of Christians I know.

In my humble opinion, Ms. Med is an authentic Southern Belle. She is always dressed to the nines, her hair is always done, her jewelry always matches her outfits, and she carries herself in a way that commands respect. One of her spiritual gifts is hospitality, and it is evident because she loves hosting get-togethers at her house. For many years, our church had our annual fish fry at the Anschultz's home. And boy, can she cook! People always ask what she brought to our church's potlucks because we know it is going to be delicious. Several years ago, she even wrote a cookbook, and I am honored to have a copy.

Ms. Med came up to me and said, "I want to talk to you after class tonight." To which I responded, "Yes ma'am," because there is no other possible response. When Ms. Med asks you to do something, your response should always be "Yes ma'am." After Bible class was over, Med, Lannas, my husband, Randall, and I met in our church's multi-purpose room and that's when she told me her story.

She had been diagnosed with breast cancer in 2012, and I honestly didn't remember it. She explained that the doctor who ended up performing her surgery was a phenomenal surgeon with a wonderful manner about her, and Med had felt comfortable talking with her and asking questions. This is when a God-whisper (shout, maybe?) happened.

Ms. Med pulled out a business card and said, "This is who I want you to go see, write this down." And she tapped her perfectly polished fingernail on the table as she pointed to the business card. "I want you to make an appointment with this surgeon. You don't have to have a referral; you can make your own appointment."

She continued, "She's located at the Vanderbilt Breast Center. When you are meeting with her, I want you to ask her about... now write this down" (more fingernail tapping). "I want you to ask her about the possibility of doing a lumpectomy and 'inter-operational radiation.' That is exactly what I did. I had surgery on a Thursday, stayed overnight in the hospital, and went home on Friday. I went to a funeral home visitation on Saturday and church on Sunday, and I just kept going from there."

She paused as I caught up with her, scribbling away. Then she continued, leaning in close to make sure I caught the full impact of her words. "I still had to fool with those drains and a few follow-up appointments, but it never really slowed me down." I said, "Well, no wonder why I didn't remember your diagnosis! It was barely a 'blip' to you and you kept right on going!" Then I announced, "Med, that is my prayer for myself – I want to have an experience as close to yours as possible." And she was in heartfelt agreement. I will never forget the sound of her fingernail tapping on the table. God was getting my attention in a very real way.

Ms. Med also shared with me her oncologist's contact information and told what a terrific experience she'd had with this doctor under the circumstances. She told me her oncologist went so far as to share her personal experience with her own mother's breast cancer treatment. She had an intimate point of reference to what her patients, specifically Ms. Med, were going through. That was a big comfort to her and to me as well.

On the way home from church that night, I was in shock, and to be honest, somewhat in disbelief. I couldn't believe what had just happened. Well, I could, but I was totally surprised. I started crying and said to Randall, "How is that for guidance and clarity?! You can't get much clearer than that!" It was an answer to my prayer. One of so many prayers.

The next day, Thursday, August 30, I had a follow-up appointment with my doctor to get the results of the MRI and to discuss how I wanted to move forward in treatment. We talked about the MRI findings first. Next, she asked me if I had decided what I wanted to do. All I said was, "I want a second opinion" and handed her the piece of scrap paper with my notes from the night before from my conversation with Ms. Med.

It had the facility name, address, phone number, and the doctors' names. She looked at it and said, "Okay. We will put a call in to them for you." She made a copy of my paper and that was that. I felt such a sense of peace about it all because I knew God was overseeing this entire operation, both literally and figuratively. I had another mammogram and ultrasound done on September 4, and my first appointment with the recommended surgeon and oncologist was scheduled for September 19.

Once my appointments had been made, God provided more whispers of confirmation that I was on the path He chose. After Sunday school class one morning, Elisa Beth Brown asked who I was going to use for my surgery. When I told her who it was, she exclaimed, "That's who I go to. You will love her!" She then went on to explain to me that she'd had a mammogram that was a bit concerning and the doctor would not let her leave until she could do a few more tests. Once she knew for certain it wasn't anything that needed more attention, she let her go home.

Another morning, Randall and I arrived at church and were getting out of our car. A different friend, Melissa Jackson, was also getting out of her car and called out to me to wait a second. She said, "I just want to hug you!" to which I replied, "And I want you to hug me." She asked where I was going for my medical care. I told her where it was and she said, "Oh I love that place! They will take great care of you. I go there and so does my momma." I felt God was involved and used them to comfort me regarding the decision to use the surgeon who was recommended by Ms. Med.

My medical team

I was grateful that my general surgeon, the oncologist, and the plastic surgeon were under one roof and worked together as a team. That was extremely convenient. They always worked their schedules so that I could make a trip to the office and see them all in one day, since it was a bit of a drive for me.

My first introduction to the medical team was the general surgeon's nurse, Ms. Carol. She is gifted in her role as a nurse. She was very comforting when she spoke with Randall and me. She would make some comments to lift my spirits at every visit, remarking on how vibrant and pretty my blue top was, or how my pedicure looked so nice, or my shoes were cute. The little things like that, showing her kindness and caring demeanor, had a lasting impact on me.

The general surgeon was similar to Ms. Carol in that she was soft-spoken and did her best to comfort me. She took her time to listen to my concerns and gave me things to think about that I had not considered. We discussed where my tumor was located and what options were available. As instructed by Ms. Med, I asked about the possibility of having a lumpectomy with inter-operational radiation. She explained that if I did a lumpectomy, I would have to follow up with radiation because of where my tumor was located. Between removing the tumor, ensuring there was a clear margin and then having radiation, she knew that my breast would be distorted and an irregular shape. She was confident that I would not be happy with the result. We agreed that the best choice for me was to do a mastectomy.

On October 3, I met with the plastic surgeon. He was very helpful in explaining the procedure, and that he would step in to perform his part when the surgeon was finished with her part of the process. That way, I would be under anesthesia once. Very clever, I thought. He drew pictures so I understood exactly what was going to take place during the surgery. He also gave me a website where I could go and look at his past 'work' and look at reviews. As weird as that sounds, I wanted to know what I was getting for my money, so to speak. I also looked around other websites for reviews on his work, and I felt comfortable that he was the right choice to perform my plastic surgery.

I met with my general surgeon again on October 5. A lot happened to me between my October 3 appointment with my plastic surgeon and October 5. I suffered a lot of inner turmoil, both mentally and emotionally. Poor Randall. He didn't know what to do with me. I was a hot mess. I went from hoping for a lumpectomy, to having a game plan with the surgeon for a single mastectomy, and now I was considering a bilateral mastectomy because I was angry. Very angry.

I decided that I was over this whole thing; I wanted it done. I wanted to have both breasts removed because I never wanted to go through this ever again. EVER! My mind was made up and I was determined.

I marched in to the see the surgeon and told her just that. I was done with it all, and I wanted to have both breasts removed because I was not going to do this again. Bless her heart. I came at her with both barrels and the look of confusion she had on her face told me she had no idea what had just happened. She looked at me, then looked at Randall, then looked back at me and said, "What is going on? I thought we had a game plan for a single mastectomy."

Randall chimed in, "That's what I've been trying to tell her!" The surgeon turned to me very calmly asked, "Okay. Okay, please explain what you're thinking? Why do you want to have both breasts removed?"

Now, with tears, I told her that I really, REALLY didn't want to go through this again. She quietly explained to me that removing the left breast did not increase my survival rate since the cancer was contained in the right breast. Then she said, "Let's do this. We have a geneticist on staff here who works with patients all the time. How about I see if she has time to talk to you. You can tell her what you are feeling and see if she can help you determine if there is a risk of the cancer coming back. Would that put your mind at ease?" Indeed, it would. Another God-whisper occurred – the geneticist was actually free to talk to us right then. Usually, you had to make an appointment and wait, but she was available.

Randall and I went down the hallway to meet with the geneticist and review my family's medical history. We talked about the women on both sides of my family who were also diagnosed with breast cancer. We talked about other medical issues, such as lung cancer, asthma, COPD, and congestive heart failure.

The consult was very enlightening, and she urged me to keep an eye on my heart health in the future. We did a mouth swab and she sent it off for analysis. It took about two and a half weeks for the result to come back. As it turned out, I was not at a higher risk for the breast cancer to return. So, we agreed to go back to the original plan of a single mastectomy with reconstruction. Surgery was scheduled for November 1, approximately five weeks after my breast cancer diagnosis was confirmed.

Surgery and the road to recovery

The night before surgery, my parents called to tell me they loved me and that, even though they were not able to be there with me in person, they were certainly there with me in spirit. They told me that they had prayed for me and would continue to do so. The call was so special to me and got me ready to face the next day.

We had to leave the house bright and early the morning of my operation. The whole way to the hospital my phone was blowing up – so many people texted me, wanted to let me know that they loved me, they were thinking of me, praying for me, and asked for Randall to update everyone as soon as he could. Then I saw a rainbow in the sky. It was not raining! But there it was, faint as it was, a small rainbow between two clouds. I took a picture. Another God-whisper that He was with me.

When Randall and I got to the hospital, we did the normal check-in at the front desk and sat down in the waiting room. It wasn't long and I was called back to get changed into the hospital gown, start the IV, and all the other 'fun' stuff they do prior to an operation. I was so surprised, but then again, I wasn't surprised, when I picked up my hospital gown to change into. *It was purple.* My favorite color.

Again, God was right there, and He was assuring me that He was by my side. I remember being in the room as I waited for them to take me back for surgery and I felt such a sense of peace. I wasn't nervous about what was about to happen. I was surprised, honestly, at how calm I actually felt.

Surgery went well and there were no surprises, all thanks and praise to the Lord Almighty! I was groggy when

I woke up, but I remember Randall leaning over me, hugging me as best he could, and saying, "It wasn't in your lymph nodes." Thank you, Lord! As you can imagine, that was such a relief for me. Another prayer answered as I had hoped it would be.

The nurse taking care of me post-surgery looked like a sweet friend of mine who I play Bunco with, Kelly Day, and I was comforted by that. I think that was another God-whisper. She asked me if I was hungry, and I was. Starving, as a matter of fact. She offered chicken noodle soup and that sounded yummy. I ended up having two bowls of soup. I told her, "I don't know what that is, but it is the best soup I've had in a long time."

She laughed and said, "It's just Campbells, straight out of the can. I warmed it up in the microwave." It hit the spot! I was released to go home within 24 hours of arriving for surgery.

Recovery went smoothly, all things considered. I had to sleep on my back for several weeks, which was challenging for me because I am a side sleeper. Randall and I worked together to log how much fluid my drains had collected and emptied them regularly. I started taking an oral medication on a daily basis.

I had weekly appointments with my plastic surgeon for six weeks while he worked on preparing my body for the final reconstruction surgery that was going to occur months later. I had follow-up appointments with my surgeon and my oncologist two weeks after surgery. I felt extremely blessed and grateful that everything went as expected and I just waited for my body to heal.

Support and love shown to me

When we announced my diagnosis, people reached out to me on so many different levels, and each one had a special impact. So many prayers went up on my behalf, and I truly felt every one of them.

Anytime someone we care for is struggling, we want to show them that we love them and want to support them. I was shown this support in many ways, and I would like to share a few of them with you. It may give you some ideas of how you can show someone that you care while they are going through a rough patch.

My immediate family was incredibly compassionate and understanding through it all. I don't know what I would have done if that wasn't the case. Anything I needed, all I had to do was ask. I can't put into words how much that meant to me.

My parents were so worried about me, but they never let it show. I can't imagine what it must have been like to be in their shoes; having a child diagnosed with cancer. They were my anchor the whole time.

My children Cash and Amy Wilson, Micah (Wilson Medrano, and Jack Kelley helped out too. I had a special treat from them waiting for me when I got home from the hospital. There was a bouquet of purple flowers, a bouquet of Twix candy bars and a six-pack of Coke (two of my favorites!. Cash and Amy also gifted me a necklace with a pendant that said, "Be still and know. Ps. 46:10." I don't know if they knew it, but it has always been one of my favorite verses.

My daughter, Micah, sent me beautiful flowers. I love getting flowers. There is so much beauty in the vibrant colors, the different flower shapes, and their fragrances. I think flowers are one of God's gifts to us that we can enjoy time and again. And knowing my favorite color, there was usually a purple flower or a purple vase involved. Another God-whisper, letting me know He was with me.

My youngest son, Jack, was very supportive of me on the home front by helping out around the house, getting me something to eat or drink while I recovered, and providing an endless supply of hugs. It may have seemed like something small to him at the time, but he was a big help.

I received several pieces of jewelry that had inspiring sentiments on them. I belong to a group of girlfriends who I have been close with since elementary school. We were fortunate to get together for supper just before my surgery. One of the girls, Heather Hughes, surprised us after we ate and said, "I brought gifts for everyone." Another girl, Cindy Stinnett, laughed and said, "I did, too!"

What was so cool about it was that Heather gave us all necklaces that said, 'Sisterhood' on them and Cindy gave us all bracelets that had '#Sisterhood' stamped on them. They had not told the other one what they were doing, so it was heartwarming that their gifts were so similar. I wore both the necklace and the bracelet all the time, because I felt like my tribe was with me when I had them on.

A colleague of mine, Doreen Williams-Holmes, gave me a bracelet that said, "Walk By Faith" and I wore it constantly. I would take such comfort in knowing my faith, and my God, were going to get me through the unknowns. I also received a bracelet that read, "I am an Overcomer" from Stephanie Lindsey and her daughter Sammie, which I wore constantly as well.

I was also given some musical CDs to enjoy. Music soothes my soul on several levels. I appreciated being given something I could listen to and quietly think about the life that was going on around me. Or I could sing along at the top of my lungs when I was alone in the car, agreeing with every word being sung. I received the Mandisa CD, that went with the bracelet, which included the song "Overcomer." I played that song over and over and over again. What encouragement I received from the words of that song!

I was given another set of CDs to listen to that had been "compiled." I think there were 5 or 6 CDs in a homemade case made of notebook paper. It was torn in several places and taped back together. Terri Cleaver, another friend from church, gave them to me. She told me, "I started to make a new case for them, one that wasn't torn up. But I decided that was part of their story." She had received the CDs months earlier from a friend of hers when she needed some encouragement.

Terri told me that I was to keep the CDs for as long as I needed them, to listen to them as often as I wanted to. But, when the time came, I was instructed to pass them along to someone else in need, and that's what I did. The person I gave them to ended up keeping them for about a year and then passed them along to someone else who could use encouragement. What a terrific idea.

I also was blessed by the number of cards I received. I think I still have every single one. They were from family members, friends, coworkers, and church members. I think my favorite cards have been the lovely handmade cards from some of the children at church. I can't tell you how special those cards are to me. All the cards brought a lot of joy. I would look at them over and over, and think about each person who sent it to me. I would think about how I knew them and the way they were involved in my life. I have been richly blessed by my friendships. Knowing people cared enough to let me know they were thinking about me and praying for me lifted my spirits when I was down. It seems that sending cards is a dying art and that is unfortunate, because such a small thing like a note or a card can mean so much.

Jenna Aikins, another co-worker in my office gifted me with a journal. At the time, I didn't realize how important the journal would become. I was able to write down, well... anything. I could write about a recent doctor visit. I could jot down a scripture that was on my heart. I was able to write about how I was feeling. In large part, writing in that journal was how the outline of this book was developed. And it was a way I could express myself privately.

I was gifted with several blankets. One was crocheted with granny squares made by a previous coworker's mother. Another colleague, Janie Pruitt, screen-printed "Be Still and Know" with a pink ribbon on a blanket. That was special to me because she had no idea that it is one of my favorite verses.

I also received another special blanket from Crystal and Patrick Folker, cherished friends of mine. It was a prayer blanket. It wasn't a full-size one, but was more like a lap blanket. A local church has a ministry where the members of the ministry team make these wonderful blankets. The whole time they are creating these treasures they are praying over them and praying for whoever the recipient will be. God already knows who it will be, and He knows their situation.

There was a card included that explained how the blanket had been prayed over and the name of the maker. I loved it because it had purple in the pattern, and it was small enough I could take it with me to the hospital. I covered up with it prior to surgery and afterwards. I literally felt covered in prayer. How incredible is that?! One of my Sisterhood friends, Laurie McCombs, has the blanket her mother was gifted when she was ill with mesothelioma. Instead of it being crocheted, her blanket is square and has fringes. The fringes are tied with small knots. Since it was small like a shawl or a lap blanket, she was able to take it with her when she had to fly or travel for treatments. I think most people can make the knotted kind of blanket – even the non-crafters. If your church is looking for an outreach, or a ministry, this may be an option.

Every year, one of our local hospitals puts on a 10K run/5K walk Classic in October. In 2018, the same year I was diagnosed, they chose to support Breast Cancer Awareness. Some of my runner friends told me they were going to sign up to run in my honor. It meant so much to me! Several of us agreed to do the walk (because we aren't runners! that was scheduled later that morning. Patrick came up with our slogan: #runliketheWendi.

Stephanie made our shirts – purple shirts with a sneaker designed from pink ribbons on the front with "Think Pink and Walk Proud" as the sole of the shoe, and the slogan on the back. To say the least, I was honored and humbled by their thoughtfulness and willingness to do this on my behalf. The day of the race, October 13, 2018, was cold and dreary, but the energy and excitement of everyone there was undeniable. There were so many people wanting to support breast cancer awareness and research. It was amazing!

I was in the area, along with all the other walkers, getting ready for the 5K to begin. Everyone was gathering around and waiting for the horn to blow. Then, out of the corner of my left eye, I saw a childhood friend approaching me. I hadn't seen her in years! Turns out she was one of the many volunteers who helped organize the 10K/5K Classic that year. We gave a quick hug and she asked me how I was doing. I honestly didn't know she knew of my diagnosis, so I gave the generic "I'm good" answer.

She then started asking me about my breast cancer diagnosis and treatment plans. I told her who my general surgeon, plastic surgeon, and oncologist were. She then shared with me a story of her aunt who had also had breast cancer. She went to the same plastic surgeon who was going to perform my reconstruction surgery! The same one! Again, a God-whisper – yet another confirmation that I was doing the right thing and on the right path. And once again, I felt God's presence with me.

I was blessed by having support shown to me by my friends and family in so many different ways. Randall was able to go with me to the majority of my doctor's appointments. He actually took great pride in referring to himself as my 'driver.' It has always been our thing – he likes to drive anywhere we go, and I like to be chauffeured. So, it works for us.

Randall has to travel some with his job, and he wasn't going to be able to take me to one of my appointments. My sweet 'Unkie' George stepped up and offered to drive me. I appreciated the gesture because I don't like to drive in heavy city traffic and it also gave us an opportunity to have one-on-one time and get caught up with each other. Plus, he understood some of the behind the scenes of things since he supported his wife, my Aunt Mary Ann, through her breast cancer experience.

We were enjoying our ride, telling stories and having a good conversation, when all of a sudden, Unkie George said, "Just so you know, I'm not going back there with you." I laughed out loud and said, "That's fine. I don't want you going back there with me." And the conversation kept going, never missing a beat. You've got to find humor wherever you can!

No man shall be able to
stand before you
all the days of your life.
Just as I was with Moses,
so I will be with you.
I will not leave you
or forsake you.

Joshua 1:5 ESV

CHAPTER 2

YOU ARE NOT ALONE

There are many women and men who have faced a diagnosis of breast cancer. The American Cancer Society website estimates breast cancer in men in the United States for 2022 are about 2,710 new cases of invasive breast cancer will be diagnosed and about 530 men will die from it.[1] Men, if you have a history of breast cancer in your family, you should get regular exams, the same as women.

I'm sure it isn't surprising that women have greater odds of being diagnosed with breast cancer. The website www.breastcancer.org states, "In 2022, an estimated 287,850 new cases of invasive breast cancer are expected to be diagnosed in women in the U.S., along with 51,400 new cases of non-invasive (in situ) breast cancer."[2]

When you are given bad news or you are facing a difficult situation, you need a support system. This can include people who love you and want to be there to listen to you when you want to voice concerns, celebrate small victories, or simply sit beside you as you quietly process the world you are currently living in. Mainly though, I looked to God to carry me through whatever was in front of me.

Your support group can also include friends who have been through a similar situation. They can walk with you through your journey with an understanding that inexperienced friends cannot. Breast cancer patients and breast cancer survivors make up our own tribe. We have our own community that those not a part of it may not fully understand.

Once word gets out that you have breast cancer, it's likely folks you didn't even know were cancer survivors will check on you and ask how they can support you. At least that was my experience. They wanted to help me through the difficult process of being diagnosed, treatment options, physician options, etc., but most importantly they wished to share with me their experience in hopes of easing my anxieties. We are always more apprehensive when there are unknowns, and I appreciated that my friends wanted to calm my fears and assure me they were available if I needed anything.

I work at a local university and it is sort of a small-town community of its own. One of my colleagues, Masako Barnaby, stopped by my office to chat with me when she heard that I had been diagnosed. She shared her experience with me, and said to me, "Of all of the cancers to get, I'm glad it was breast cancer. There is more known about breast cancer than so many other cancers. They are always doing research and the advancements they have made, just in the last few years, is incredible."

Masako asked me if I was going to have chemotherapy. At that time, I was unsure as my medical team and I were still developing a plan. She had a great suggestion that she wanted to pass along to me, just in case I was going to need chemo. This advice was given to her prior to her chemotherapy treatments.

Masako explained that when she was diagnosed, it was suggested to her to go shopping for a wig *before* treatment began. She explained to me where our local American Cancer Society was located and said they offered wigs for breast cancer patients. She told me to go while I still had my hair because they would be able to match my current hair color and style. Or I could get something completely different. (If you have always wanted to be a redhead, now is your chance! Ha!) She explained that if you are able to shop for your wigs before you *need* them, it makes the experience much more enjoyable (as much as you can enjoy it under the circumstances).

I would never have thought of that! I appreciated her wisdom and her willingness to share it with me. If you find yourself in a situation where you will be looking for a wig, maybe make a 'date' of it with a girlfriend, sister, mom, or daughter. While out shopping, grab lunch and take it to the park to eat, for example. This would also be a great time to update your pajama wardrobe! Pajama tops that button in the front are your friends because you probably will not be able to lift your arms for some time while you heal from surgery. Think about your shirts, too. You may need to get a few shirts that button in the front so you can get dressed more easily.

Allow yourself to feel ALL the emotions

Allow yourself to feel ALL the emotions because there will be plenty, and they can bubble up out of nowhere. Allow yourself time to process your diagnosis. Give yourself permission to grieve because it's likely that life as you knew it will be forever changed. It came out of nowhere and you didn't have time to prepare. And your 'new normal' is a bit off in the distance yet, so there is uncertainty there. Be sad. Be angry. Be scared. Be determined. Be weak. Be strong. Be quiet. Scream. All of it. Whatever you need to feel, feel it. Your world has just been turned upside down. It's a lot to take in, so take the time you need to catch your breath. This is your journey down this path, and it is as individual as you are. Set your own pace.

Look for God

Now, maybe more than ever, is the time for you to turn your focus to God. Be purposeful in looking for God's whispers; signs that He is with you. He wants to connect with you in a very real and tangible way and this is a terrific opportunity for you to open doors to God, allowing Him to bond with you on a very specific and personal level. Think about something that means a lot to you – a favorite scent, a favorite color, or something you like to collect.

For example, if your favorite flower is a rose, your favorite candy is chocolate, or if you have a collection of spoons – whatever it is – embrace those thoughts and memories. When something holds a special meaning to you, you know why, and so does God. He will use it to whisper to you.

About the time I received my diagnosis, I was in a ladies' Bible class at church. It was on a Wednesday night and Stephanie was teaching the class. She shared that her mother, Becky Folker, passed away when she was young. Her mother became sick with lung cancer, despite never having smoked, and it eventually spread to her brain.

Becky loved angels. It didn't matter if it was a picture of an angel, a figurine, or a print. Becky's children think she developed a love, understanding, and appreciation for angels when she taught a series on angels for her ladies' class at church.

Stephanie explained to our class what Becky's room looked like. There were angel figurines on the mantel and on the coffee table. Everywhere you looked were angels! One of her favorite pieces was a painting of an angel that her son, Patrick, did. It hung on the wall where she could see it from her bed. People wanted Becky to know that they were thinking of her, that they loved her, and that they were praying for her. They did so by giving her gifts of angels. Becky felt God's presence and His angels watching over her!

I took the story to heart and thought to myself, "My favorite color is purple. I'm going to look for things that are purple." I told God, as if He didn't already know, "Every time

I see something purple, I'm going to think of You. I'm going to know that is You letting me know that You are right beside me, walking this journey with me."

My scavenger hunt for purple began, and it was everywhere. It was almost as if purple things – those God-whispers- were looking for me! It might be hard to believe, but it is true. For example, remember Jenna, my coworker who got me a journal for writing anything I felt the need to put down on paper? She ordered it in pink, thinking of the Breast Cancer Awareness ribbon. But the journal arrived and it was purple!

I received purple flowers on several occasions, or flowers in purple vases, and I was also gifted a blanket that had purple in the design. I could go on, but you get the idea. The more I looked for purple things, the more pronounced it was to see. And it was such a comfort to me. I encourage you to be intentional and actively look for signs that God is with you.

Attitude goes a LONG way

I am a long-time believer in 'you find what you look for.' I'm sure you have known some people who have a reputation for being negative. Those people tend to find the negative in any situation, don't they? If they were given $100, they would complain that it wasn't $200. And positive people tend to find the silver lining in any situation. If their car broke down and the repair bill is $200, they would be thankful it wasn't more expensive.

Your attitude toward your situation can go a long way toward the success of your treatment and recovery. There are so many studies out there that illustrate how a positive attitude can increase your odds for success.

With so much out of your control, one thing you are able to manage to some extent is your overall environment. Surround yourself with positivity as much as possible. Be purposeful about it. Just after receiving my diagnosis, I decided I needed to have positive influences all around me as consistently as was feasible. For example, when folks asked me, "What can I do to help?" I told them to be normal. While my world had a bit of a 'bump in the road', life goes on. I wanted to hear what was going on in their lives and that it was okay to talk to me about their health issues.

I told them that Randall and I made an agreement that we would continue our lives as normally as possible, because that would help us manage the 'not normal' part of our lives. Then I said, "Be positive. If you catch yourself having a negative attitude or making negative comments, stop it. I need positivity in my life!" And, of course, I asked for their prayers.

Others will lean on you

I was a bit surprised by this fact. I found myself, time and again, having to assure others that everything was going to be okay. After talking to other breast cancer survivors, it seems to be a common theme. I'm not really sure why that is, either. It reminded me of the scenario when a child is learning to walk, and they stumble and fall. The baby looks at their parents and studies their reaction to decide if they should cry or not.

People in my circles looked to me for guidance on how they should respond. I believed I had to be strong for them.

So, I was. I felt an obligation to be there and support them, because that's what moms, wives, children, and friends do. I also felt like my faith was being tested and I wanted to lead by example of me leaning on God as I weathered this storm. And it was truly through God that I found my strength.

Be honest

You have to be honest with your family and friends. Tell them what you need and when you need it. Those around you want to help you in any way that they can. It's likely they feel a bit (or a lot) helpless. Let them bless you by helping you. This goes from the time you receive your diagnosis all the way through the last days of treatment and beyond. Perhaps a way will present itself that you can pay it forward someday.

It is rare that I ask anyone for help. Personally, I have an issue with feeling like I am imposing on others. It has been a thorn in my side all my life. But I was forced to put that aside and ask for help on several occasions during this time. I remember feeling so heavy-hearted after receiving my diagnosis. I would tell Randall that I wasn't up to cooking supper, so he would cook that night or go pick up something at a drive-thru.

Sometimes, you may be tired and not up for visitors. You may have to tell your family, friends, and neighbors that, while you appreciate the gesture, you just need to rest. Usually, they will be understanding. If they aren't, that's okay. You have to take care of *you*. Friends and family love you and want what is best for you. It is up to you to let them know what that is.

Journal your experience

Writing stuff down and documenting details helped me as I went through the breast cancer process. My journal is the foundation of this book. You don't have to have elaborate entries. I certainly didn't. I wrote down notes, as well as bits and pieces as things happened or as I remembered them. You can write down your feelings or your thoughts about a particular doctor's appointment. Maybe jot down something you've researched about your treatment options. If a friend stops by for a visit and brings a gift, record how that made you feel and what the gift was.

Keeping a journal is an important piece that will allow you to look back over your journey and reflect. When you are feeling down, it can boost your spirits seeing, "Barbara came by today and brought me a card with some cookies." You might even want to designate a section of your journal for 'feel-good' entries, favorite scriptures, or positive quotes. You will appreciate reading them often.

Your doctors' visits

You will be given a lot of information in a short amount of time, especially after diagnosis. It is difficult to comprehend everything you are being told. I suggest taking a small notebook with you to your appointments and jotting down what you can. And don't be afraid to ask the nurse or physician to repeat what they just said. Some of the words being used sound like Greek to those of us who are nonmedical people, so be sure to clarify anything you are confused about. Then take your notes home and look them over and over again. Take time to digest it all and understand what is going on with your body and what options are available.

Also, if possible, have someone go with you to each of your doctor appointments, especially for the initial visits when you and your medical team are developing a treatment plan. It is helpful to have a second set of ears listening to everything that is being said as they may catch something that you missed. You may even consider asking the doctor if you can record your conversations during your appointments. You can then replay them later, giving you the option to listen to the discussion again.

I was very fortunate to have a terrific team of physicians, surgeons, and nurses. They were very thorough with explaining my diagnosis and my options. I was shown the scans so I could see exactly where the tumor was located. They were willing to answer any question I had, which honestly weren't very many because I felt like I didn't even know enough to know what to ask. I thought it might be helpful to make a list of some things for you to consider talking over with your doctor. Some questions may not have an answer until after surgery. Another list is located in the back of the book (Appendix A), with space for answers. Feel free to make a copy and take it to your doctors' appointments.

Diagnosis

- What type of cancer do I have?
- Is it an aggressive type?
- Where is the tumor located?
- How big is the tumor?
- What stage is the tumor?
- Is the cancer in my lymph nodes?

- What is my estrogen receptor (ER) and progesterone receptor (PR) status?
  - Ask your doctor for a more complete definition, but a general definition for estrogen receptor (ER) is a protein found inside the cells of the female reproductive tissue, some other types of tissue, and some cancer cells. The hormone estrogen will bind the receptors inside the cells and may cause the cell to grow[3].
  - Ask your doctor for a more complete definition, but a general definition for progesterone receptor (PR) is a protein found inside the cells of the female reproductive tissue, some other types of tissue, and some cancer cells. The hormone progesterone will bind to the receptors inside the cells and may cause the cells to grow[3].
- What is my HER2 status?
  - Ask your doctor for a more complete definition, but a general definition for HER2 is a protein involved in normal cell growth. HER2 may be made in larger than normal amounts by some types of cancer cells, including breast, ovarian, bladder, pancreatic, and stomach cancers. This may cause cancer cells to grow more quickly and spread to other parts of the body. Checking the amount of HER2 on some types of cancer cells may help plan treatment[3].
  - HER2 Negative – Describes cells that have a small amount or none of a protein called HER2 on their surface. In normal cells, HER2 helps control cell growth. Cancer cells that are HER2 negative may grow more slowly and are less

31

likely to recur (come back) or spread to other parts of the body than cancer cells that have a large amount of HER2 on their surface. Checking to see if a cancer is HER2 negative may help plan treatment. Cancers that may be HER2 negative include breast, bladder, ovarian, pancreatic, and stomach cancers[3].

o HER2 Positive – Describes cells that have a protein called HER2 on their surface. In normal cells, HER2 helps control cell growth. Cancer cells that make too much HER2 may grow more quickly and are more likely to spread to other parts of the body. Checking to see if a cancer is HER2 positive may help plan treatment, which may include drugs that kill HER2-positive cancer cells. Cancers that may be HER2 positive include breast, bladder, pancreatic, ovarian, and stomach cancers[3].

- Is a port recommended for treatment so repeated needle sticks won't be necessary?
- Should I be concerned with being immune-compromised? If so, how will that be handled?

Surgery

- If surgery is the best option, do you recommend a lumpectomy? Mastectomy?
- Will any lymph nodes be removed during surgery?
- How much clear margin is expected?
- What type of bandages/drains will be used?
- How invasive is the surgery?
- Can anything be saved?

- o I suggest this question because after a conversation with both my general surgeon and plastic surgeon, it was determined the nipple could be saved. Honestly, that was a game-changer for me. I was so fortunate that my medical team was very good about communicating with each other.
- Is reconstruction surgery an option? If so, when would it be done?

Implants

- Are implants wanted/necessary?
- Is it possible for both the general surgeon and the plastic surgeon to work together during one surgery?
- If I am having a single mastectomy, do you suggest getting an implant on the other side as well, for symmetry?
- Does the plastic surgeon recommend saline or silicone implants?
- Is there an expiration date on the implants?
- Does the plastic surgeon have photos of other patients so I could see their work?
- If I lose or gain weight after the surgery, will it affect the look of the implants/breasts?

Treatment

- What are the treatment options: Chemo? Radiation? An oral medication like Tamoxifen?
- If I have been through or am going through menopause, does that make a difference in my treatment options?

- If radiation is necessary, what is the preparation procedure?
- How long will this process take before my first radiation treatment?
- How will they know where to administer the radiation?

Recovery

- What is the time period for treatment and medication?
- If it is necessary to take time off from work, how long is recovery expected to take?
- What restrictions will I have?
- Will I have to adjust how I sleep?
- Will I need to have physical therapy following surgery?
  - o This one surprised me because I wasn't expecting to have physical therapy following a mastectomy surgery. However, it was necessary because I was restricted in how high I could raise my arm for weeks after surgery. Once everything had healed enough, I began PT to be able to raise my arm over my head again.)

Here is a space for you to write your own questions:

_____

_____

_____

_____

_____

_____

_____

_____

_____

Your spouse/partner is walking with you

I encourage you to be mindful of your spouse/partner during this time. Understand they are with you as you navigate through the breast cancer world, but in a different way. They want to show you support but may be not quite sure how to do that. And you may not be quite sure what to tell them, either. At times they are likely to feel helpless, but they hurt alongside you.

When I was going through the process of my breast cancer diagnosis and was researching what treatment options were available, we met with so many doctors in such a short period of time. We were talking to my oncologist several weeks after my initial diagnosis, and she was providing information for the medication I would be taking following surgery. She explained what I should watch for in the medicine's side effects.

It was then Randall asked her, "You mean this is curable?" She said, "Yes! Absolutely!" I could literally see the weight being lifted off his shoulders from the relief he felt. As we were leaving the office, he turned to me in the hallway, with tears in his eyes, and said, "This what I have been waiting to hear this whole time. You are going to make it."

His comment hit me like a ton of bricks! It wasn't until that moment I realized what *he* had been going through this entire time. It honestly never occurred to me that I wasn't going to be okay, but he was struggling with the possibility that he might lose his wife. And of course, he wasn't going to talk about that to me. He wanted to be strong for my sake. It still breaks my heart knowing how he suffered in silence.

Your children are walking with you, too

I also encourage you to be mindful of your children during this time, too. They probably aren't included in the doctors' visits and all of those conversations, so keep them informed as best you can of the status of things. Let them know what the results of doctors' appointments are, what decisions have been made, a timeline of when they can expect things to happen, etc., as much as possible. They may need some extra attention during this time. Their mother is going through a lot and they likely feel helpless as well. There are a lot of scary unknowns all around them, too.

Younger children will likely have a lot of questions and have trouble understanding what is happening. Take the time to explain what is going on in words they can grasp. My children were older (senior in high school and late 20s) so I was able to share with them most everything that was discussed with the doctors. Randall and I decided to tell them about my diagnosis when we had an idea what the game plan was going to be. We knew they were going to have concerns and we wanted to be able to address them with as much information as possible.

Don't forget about yourself

I also want to encourage you to be mindful of yourself. Self-care is extremely important. Your body is going through a lot during treatments and recovery. Take time out for yourself to do something you enjoy. It may be simply sitting out on the back patio drinking morning coffee or going for a long car ride listening to your favorite songs blaring on the radio. Make an appointment to get a mani/pedi. Read the Bible. Pray – anything that can lift your spirits and make you feel like you have a chance to breathe.

Also, take your vitamins and drink plenty of water. Consider having some protein shakes on hand. Protein helps your body heal. Sometimes when you don't have an appetite or aren't really in the mood for a meal, a protein shake may be a good alternative. Give your body as much ammunition as you can as it recovers. Also, check with your doctors to see if they have any suggestions to help your body as it heals.

Think about getting professionally fitted for a bra. If you've had a lumpectomy or mastectomy, a regular bra may be uncomfortable now. There are a lot of varieties and options available. Your insurance will likely cover several new bras a year. Your surgeon or physician can write a prescription for them.

And girl let me tell you – you are allowed to have a pity party every once in a while! I hope you have some ice cream, lots of chocolate, and all the carbs you want! Binge watch some of your favorite shows and eat all the junk food your belly can hold.   It's okay to allow yourself some time to wallow around in it for a bit. But don't stay there too long. Pull up your bootstraps and move along.

Rejoice in hope, be patient in tribulation, be constant in prayer.

Romans 12:12 ESV

CHAPTER 3

LET PEOPLE BLESS YOU

I want to start this section off by addressing the patient, specifically. As I mentioned before, I have struggled my entire life with avoiding the feeling of being a burden to someone or imposing on others. During my surgery and recovery, it was exceptionally challenging for me to allow others to 'do' for me. It goes against every fiber of my being and is very uncomfortable. When folks would ask me what I needed or how they could help, I would always respond with, "I'm fine," or "We're good." However, I was inwardly grateful when some of my close friends ignored me and 'did' anyway.

We used to have a next-door neighbor, Ms. Lockhart, who was up in years but very independent. We kept an eye on her and wanted to help her with things we noticed she might need done around her house. In one particular instance, we noticed a limb down in her yard as we were leaving to run some errands. When we came home a few hours later, she was in the yard with a handsaw trying to cut it up.

Randall got out of the car and fussed at her, telling her he was going to do that for her but hadn't had the chance yet. So, we brought the groceries in the house and Randall went to cut up the limb for her. She offered him some money for helping, and he said, "You're going to get me in trouble with my wife. She told me not to take anything from you." She then came looking for me. I tried to refuse the money, explaining to her that we were just being neighborly, but she wasn't having it. She giggled, threw the money at me, and ran away as fast as she could.

My sweet husband explained it to me this way. He said by not allowing her to give us something in return for our help, we were robbing her of her ability to bless someone. I never thought if it that way before. It made sense.

All of that to say, if you are the one going through hardship, let others bless you and do for you. God may be using them for a purpose greater than you and your situation. Don't rob them of that opportunity. If people who care for you want to help you – let them.

How can you help?

As a spouse/partner, family member, or friend, how can you help? When someone is going through a difficult time, most of us have an automatic response of "Let me know what I can do." It's one of the things we say to show that we care about them. It's our default response when we don't know what to do, but we want to make the offer in case the struggling person comes up with something we can do, because we are ready to respond. But when your loved one is experiencing illness or difficulty, they may not know themselves how someone can help them. They are only trying to survive and get through the next hour, day, appointment, meal, shower, etc.

I challenge you to think of a way that you can do something that would be helpful, without waiting for a suggestion or permission from them. It doesn't have to be anything grand or expensive either. Trust me when I say the gesture itself, no matter how small or simple to you it may seem, will be greatly appreciated.

I've already mentioned a few ways that I was blessed by those around me. I want to share some other suggestions (some of which I also had the pleasure of enjoying!) that could be beneficial to your loved one.

Pray for her

First and foremost, pray. If you can do nothing else, pray to God on behalf of your loved one. The benefits of prayer are undeniable. James 5:16 (ESV) comes to mind:

> *Therefore, confess your sins to one another and pray for one another, that you may be healed. The prayer of a righteous person has great power as it is working.*

And look what happened to Peter in prison! Acts 12:5-7 (ESV) tells us:

> *So Peter was kept in prison, but earnest prayer for him was made to God by the church. Now when Herod was about to bring him out, on that very night, Peter was sleeping between two soldiers, bound with two chains, and sentries before the door were guarding the prison. And behold, an angel of the Lord stood next to him, and a light shone in the cell. He struck Peter on the side and woke him, saying "Get up quickly." And the chains fell off his hands.*

I am not saying that God will literally drop your 'chains,' but I am saying that prayer is POWERFUL. It is a tool that can make a way where a path cannot be seen. And as this example shows us, the church was praying to God on behalf of Peter, and God heard their prayers and responded.

I came across a book written by Dr. Larry Dossey called *Healing Words: The Power of Prayer and the Practice of Medicine.*[4] It is about various scientific studies done to determine if prayer, as part of the patient's treatment regime, is beneficial or not. Several components for the experiments mentioned throughout the book are:

- How to pray and what to pray for,
- The element of time (for example, when prayers are answered before they are made),

- Loving, caring, or having empathy between the person praying and the person receiving the benefits of the prayer, and
- The patients' physician's beliefs and whether or not that is a correlation to improvements on health.

Numerous laboratory experiments were reported, along with how the research was conducted, and the results were included in the book.

Dr. Dossey's book states:

> "To be sure, prayer does not need science to legitimize or justify it. Even so, I believe that if science can demonstrate the potency of prayer, people who pray are likely to feel empowered and validated in their beliefs as a result. Furthermore, using science does not always require that we 'put nature on the rack' and torture her to reveal her secrets . . . . Instead, we can honor what is being investigated and approach it with respect and reverence. From this point of view, investigating prayer does not imply 'bringing God into the laboratory,' but 'bringing the laboratory to God,' requesting and inviting the Universe to reveal its workings."

The book also describes several studies conducted with varying degrees of distances between the praying person and the one receiving prayer. It was determined that prayer was effective regardless of proximity. Whether close by or miles away, prayers for the patient were deemed successful.

Experiments were performed using subjects other than humans, as well. Things such as water, fungus, bacteria, red blood cells and plants were included in the research. These tests also demonstrated the power of prayer.

Dr. Dossey describes it this way:

"Prayer can be intrinsically helpful. This is a way of saying that prayer works positively, of itself, and that its beneficial power is not due entirely to suggestion and the placebo response.

"Evidence is abundant for an intrinsic, positive effect of prayer not only in humans but in mice, chicks, enzymes, fungi, yeast, bacteria, and cells of various sorts. We cannot dismiss these outcomes as being due to suggestion or placebo effects, since these so-called lower forms of life do not think in any conventional sense and are presumably not susceptible to suggestion."

Experiments were also conducted testing the claim that healing effects could be transmitted by secondary materials, such as praying over an object and then giving that object to the patient. This test was done by placing wool or cotton that had been prayed over into rats' cages who suffered with enlarged thyroids due to lack of iodine in their diets. The thyroid glands of the rats receiving the wool or cotton grew significantly more slowly than did the thyroid glands of the control rats. And when the rats were all returned to an iodine-containing diet, those in the cages containing the wool or cotton had thyroid glands that returned to normal size quicker than did the control rats.

I felt this firsthand. As I shared before, I was gifted a prayer blanket. The lady who crocheted it prayed over it while she worked. I honestly felt the prayers as it covered me during my time in the hospital. It was so comforting.

I think we have all heard it said before: "I can't do anything else, but I can pray for you. It's the least I can do." But actually, it is the *most* anyone can do. For any situation. Pray sincerely and often.

Let her rest

Friends and family have good intentions. They want to check in on the patient and see how she is feeling with a quick text or phone call. Does she need anything? Is she in the mood for lunch? While it is truly wonderful to have so many people show love and concern for the patient, it can disrupt rest time. It might be helpful to have someone on hand who can run interference, so to speak. Maybe this person can even take the patient's phone away for the time being, until her nap is over. It could also be nice to have someone who can meet guests at the front door if a meal is being dropped off. Allowing the patient uninterrupted rest goes a long way in the healing process.

Establish a point of contact

I suggest designating someone as a point of contact for the patient's family. This person can relay medical information or needs to others. When someone is going through the process of diagnosis and treatment, having to tell the news or share the most recent updates over and over again is exhausting. And, depending on the situation, it can be upsetting. For the patient and their family to have someone to speak to others on their behalf may be appreciated.

Goodie baskets

I was blessed with a goodie basket from my co-workers days before my surgery. It was filled with so many things that I would have never purchased for myself. The basket itself proved to be handy post-surgery, too. It contained things like a neck pillow, some sugar-free hard candies and mints, a notepad, a reusable water bottle, and a few other items. These were all very useful and I appreciated having them on hand. Some other ideas are:

Deodorant wipes
Travel-size tissues
Flexible straws
Cleansing wipes
Lip balm
Hand and body lotion
Makeup remover wipes
Hat, scarf, and/or turban
PJs with button-down tops
Comfy tops with buttons down the front
Soft cardigan sweater
Fuzzy socks
Fluffy robe
Small, round ice packs
A chest pillow
A small pillow for under the arm
A seatbelt pillow
A wedge pillow to help with sleeping
A blanket
A planner or calendar to keep up with doctor appointments
Magazines
Puzzle books and pens

Thank-you note cards and stamps

Books about anything other than breast cancer (it's nice to give your brain a break from thinking about it)

'Gift certificates' or 'coupons' for rides to follow-up appointments, picking up supper, bringing her some ice cream, etc.

Gift cards to favorite restaurants or gas for the vehicle

Snacks and/or fruit

Bottles of juice or water

Powerade or Gatorade

A journal and pen

Aquaphor Healing Ointment Advanced Therapy and/or Calendula Cream (especially helpful for radiation patients)

Appendix B has an easy-to-copy version of this suggested shopping list.

Be there

Be available for her. Sometimes just being there, physically in the moment, is all she needs. Someone to sit with her in silence while she processes the world going on around her. Having someone at home while she sleeps could give a sense of calmness and peace. On the flip side, be understanding when she needs her space and time alone. Don't take it personally. Sometimes she has been poked and prodded and scanned for this and tested for that, and she just wants to be left alone. Completely alone.

Be patient

Be patient with her emotions and with your own feelings as well. She may be happy and laughing one minute and then the next have hot flashes, bursts of anger, bursts of tears, or bursts of "I-don't-know-WHAT-I-am-feeling!" You may feel frustrated and like you are walking on eggshells around her, but she is likely more frustrated than you are and just wanting to feel 'normal' again. The moods swings are no fun for anybody.

It could be that she used to love to eat fried chicken, spaghetti, tacos, or hamburgers and fries, but her favorites aren't setting well in her stomach now. Certain medications or treatments can cause patients to have a strong metallic taste or sores in their mouths. It may end up that only one or two foods set well without making her feel nauseous. She may not eat as much as she used to for the same reason.

Allow her to recover at her own pace following surgery. There is a fine line between encouraging your loved one and pushing her. Her body has been through a lot, and it needs time to recover. And each patient's recovery is different. She may not be ready to get up and walk down the driveway two weeks post-surgery. She may be perfectly content to sit in front of the TV for weeks on end.

Unless she seems to be struggling with depression, let her be. She will get up and get moving when she feels comfortable. This includes leaving the house. While it is possible to leave the house with drains, it's not the most fun thing in the world. You feel like everyone 'knows,' and it makes a woman feel very self-conscious. It is awkward, to say the least.

She will get a shower when she is up to it, too. Understand that to her, it may be more than just getting a shower. She is going through a lot of physical adjustments, and she may dread having to undress and SEE the results of the cancer, her new normal.

Many women struggle with their identity as a woman following a lumpectomy or mastectomy, because it feels as if part of their womanhood has been taken away. It will take time to come to grips with it, so be patient in the meantime. Be supportive by telling her that you still love her, and that she is still beautiful to you, regardless of the change in her physical appearance.

Also understand that she may tire more easily and not be able to do as much as she used to, even months after surgery. It will take a long time, maybe a year or more, for her body to heal completely. She must be careful and not overdo it during that time. And she could be experiencing a side effect of her medicine. Be patient with her if she has to back out of plans at the last minute. She may need to put her feet up and rest.

Gas for her vehicle

If you are able, it would be terrific to fill up the gas tank of the vehicle she plans to take to the next doctor's appointment. Gas for the car is one of those things that we sometimes forget we need until we get in the car to go somewhere. It's a big help to get in the car heading for the doctor and not have to stop on the way to get gas, especially in the first weeks or months following surgery.

Meals

I can't say enough about meals. This was something that people helped us with, and it was so incredibly valuable. We are blessed because our church has many talents, and having people who can cook is one of them! A friend from church, Bonnie Fleischman, brought a meal over the night before my surgery, and I was so appreciative of that. How thoughtful to bring something the night <u>before</u> surgery?! It was perfect because I was so busy trying to get everything ready, I had no idea what we were going to have for supper that night. To be honest, supper hadn't even crossed my mind. She picked up a 'ready' meal from a grocery – chicken and potatoes with a ready-made salad. It was exactly what we needed.

For those of you who are cooks, homemade meals are always a hit. You might want to double-check if there are food allergies – something like nuts or gluten – that should be avoided. If you are worried about what the family may or may not like, you can always put things on the side or separate foods into different containers. Disposable containers are the best, so it doesn't matter if they aren't returned.

Another option is to utilize an online meal signup website. It is sort of like a potluck, and people sign up for what they want to take to the family. Everyone signing up can see what others are taking so there aren't duplicates. Some good ones are: perfectpotluck.com, takethemameal.com, mealtrain.com, or signupgenius.com. When you are setting up your signup sheet, think about the timing. It's a good idea to space out the meals so the family doesn't have an overabundance of food and then it goes to waste.

Of course, there is always the option of gift cards to her favorite restaurants. A good variety (burgers, chicken, Italian, Mexican, Chinese, etc.) so she can have several choices would be nice. Gift cards are very handy because you don't have to worry about them spoiling, like food, and the family can use them when it works best for their schedule.

Housecleaning help

When I was home and recovering after surgery, two of my dear friends from church, Laura Oliver and Paula Smith, came over and cleaned my house. They didn't ask me if I wanted them to; they told me when they were coming. I was hesitant at first, because I didn't want to impose on their free time, but they were insistent. To be truthful, I wasn't sure when I had really cleaned my whole house last as there had been a lot going on in the past few months. We really did appreciate their help.

If you want to help your friend as she recovers, you don't have to clean her whole house, necessarily. But you can do small things like sweep the front porch, load the dishwasher, take out the trash, or do a quick vacuum where people will be when they come to visit.

A generous gift that you, or several of your friends together, could give her is a couple of months of a housecleaning service. It doesn't have to be on a weekly basis. Once a month or every other week would be helpful because it will be several weeks before she is released from the doctor to do those types of activities herself.

Groceries

If you are running to the grocery for your weekly shopping, or to pick up one or two things quickly, it might be helpful to reach out to the family and see if they need anything. An extra treat or two thrown in the grocery bag would be a nice surprise, too. The days of the grocery 'click' lists makes things so much easier too. Once they place their online order, you could offer to swing by and pick it up for them.

Thank-you notes

Sending thank-you notes to people for showing kindness during this difficult time is an important courtesy. The patient may not be up to writing a bunch of notes, but she still wants to acknowledge what has been done for her and her family and show her appreciation. Think about buying note cards and writing inside each card a generic "Thank you for thinking of me and my family during this time." or "Thank you for allowing God to use you in order to bless us." Then she can sign the card, if she'd like. Or they can be signed on behalf of the family (The Kelley Family). Follow through, then, by placing stamps on the cards, addressing, and mailing them.

Help with the children

No doubt she will be busy with doctors' appointments and follow-ups and general dealing with the whole 'breast cancer thing.' If her children are involved in sports or other extracurricular activities, it would be helpful to drop them off and pick them up for their next practice, meet, or competition. Do they need help with homework? Do they need anything for school (clothes, supplies, etc.) that you could help with?

If your family is going on an outing together, maybe to the park, the movies or out for pizza, consider inviting her children to come along. They may appreciate a fun time with friends and a chance to get away for a little while.

Going for a drive

Sometimes there is nothing like getting out of the house for some fresh air. A wonderful way to do that is to pick her up and take her for a drive. Getting her out of the house for a bit, feeling the sun on her face, and just driving around can be so good for the soul.

Everyday stuff

Think about things you do at your house to keep things going and apply those to your friend's needs. Life just keeps going regardless of any health issues and things still have to be seen to. You could offer to: pick up or drop off their mail; pick up or drop off prescriptions at the pharmacy; do the laundry (if she's not comfortable with you personally doing the family laundry, consider dropping it off at a laundromat); make any bill payments that need to be made in person; or change bed sheets. There is nothing like getting into bed with fresh sheets. #amiright?

Special role

As a spouse or partner of a breast cancer patient, you have a special role that no one else can fill. You will see her at her worst. You will see the intimate and private side of breast cancer that isn't shown to the outside world. You need to understand that your love, care, and support is exactly what she needs during this time. She did not ask to be put in this situation, but she is able to face it with your help.

This experience will likely put added stress on your relationship. You can use this opportunity to grow closer together, or you can allow it to come between you. My prayer is you make the choice to grow closer together, as Randall and I did.

But Moses said to God, "Who am I that I should go to Pharaoh and bring the children of Israel out of Egypt?" He said, "But I will be with you..."

Exodus 3:11-12a ESV

CHAPTER 4

CONTINUE TO PUSH THROUGH AND LOOK TO GOD

Anytime I am put in a situation where I have to take charge and make decisions, I become hyper focused on getting the job done. Emotions don't have a place there. For example, when Cash, my oldest son, broke his arm, I immediately went into motion to get him medical attention as quickly as possible. I sent my daughter to a neighbor, called my parents to come get her, and then took him to the emergency room. I talked to the doctors and nurses, he had X-rays, and we learned the extent of his injury. He was fitted with a cast and we then went home. That night, when everyone was home and tucked in their beds and I knew all was going to be okay, that is when I broke down and cried. That's when I let my emotions out.

Going through my breast cancer experience was no different, although I didn't realize it at the time. Believe me when I say I experienced a lot of emotion during that time! Ups and downs galore. I thought I was processing and dealing with all the emotional and mental sides of things. And I was, to some degree. But, as I mentioned before, just as I deal with stressful situations, I had been hyper focused. I was trying to navigate through the unknown territory of breast cancer, take care of my health needs, and be strong for my family and friends during the first year.

It was the second year that *totally* caught me off guard. In that year, I started having my 'first anniversaries' of biopsies, diagnoses, and surgeries, and I experienced more emotional and mental distress than I expected. My mastectomy was behind me as well as my reconstruction surgery. I was taking my medication and I was going to be fine. Because everything was 'over' and I could relax and let my guard down, that second year was probably a harder year for me than when I was actually going through all the high drama of the cancer. Honestly. I wasn't expecting that. Not at all.

When I went for my first gynecologist visit following my surgeries, which would have been my first visit back to where I had the original test run that started it all, I almost had a panic attack sitting in the waiting room. I had flashbacks of that initial visit. I had to talk myself out of getting up and leaving. I reasoned with myself that the likelihood of them finding something, of all of that happening again, was small. I knew I was going to have to experience the first appointment sometime, so I might as well get it over with. I kept telling myself, over and over, "God is with you. God is with you. It will be fine. You are going to be fine. God is with you." I talked to God more during the second year, I think, than while I was going through everything initially. He helped me continue to heal, not just physically, but emotionally and mentally as well. God is faithful.

Make a purpose out of the pain

I said from the very beginning that I wanted to use my experience to help others. I was visualizing helping those in or close to my circle of friends and family. But God had other plans. He wanted me to reach out to share with as many people as were willing to listen about how His love and care carried me through. And how I felt Him every step of the way. It is now a part of my life story and my testimony to others. To me, it is evidence that God is there for each of us and wants to be a part of our lives. He wants to walk with us and hold us up throughout our trials. He wants us to lean on Him and look to Him for the peace and comfort that only He can provide.

Comparative suffering or survivor's remorse

Comparative suffering and survivor's remorse are very real for some cancer patients. Comparative suffering works in two ways. For example, a person who has chronic migraines feels they are experiencing more pain and misery than someone who received the wrong order at a restaurant. Conversely, a person who has chronic migraines feels they are experiencing a lesser struggle than a starving child. With this perspective, we begin to rank our pain and suffering and use it to deny or give ourselves permission to feel a certain way. It may even cause us to experience a sense of guilt if we aren't suffering as much as other people.

Personally, I felt that I had such a 'mild' case of breast cancer. I didn't have to go through horrible chemo or radiation treatments. I didn't lose my hair. I felt like my cancer was insignificant. So many women have suffered so much more than I did, and I had no right to complain about what I went through.

It was during that emotional time period that my friend Stephanie was scheduled to have a lumpectomy and then radiation treatments. I told her I felt helpless to help her. I wanted to support her, but I wasn't sure how. I didn't have to have radiation like she was going to have to endure, so I didn't feel like I was justified in telling her how to get through something I hadn't experienced myself. I mean, who was *I* to tell *her* how to get through more extensive treatment?

What she said to me next was another God-whisper and has stuck with me ever since. She said, "Wendi! Your story gives my daughter hope that everything is going to be alright. I know I'm going to be ok, but she is so concerned about me. We talk about what is going on with me, and you are an example to her that I can beat breast cancer."

At that moment, I realized that my experience was an answer to my prayer. My prayer had <u>clearly</u> been answered. Here I had been feeling like I had no business helping others because I wasn't 'sick' enough, or my cancer wasn't 'bad' enough. However, God answered my prayer – the prayer to have a similar experience to Ms. Med's. While my experience wasn't just like hers, it was really close. Praise Jesus and all glory to Him!

Survivor's remorse, or survivor's guilt, is when someone has survived a life-threating situation, like breast cancer, and others might not have. One friend chatted with me after her radiation treatments had ended. She was experiencing some pain – lightning-bolt sensations – where her radiation occurred. She shared with me that she was struggling with survivor's guilt, because a few years before that, her sister-in-law had passed away from breast cancer.

She told me that her sister-in-law only got relief from her pain by passing away, and it wasn't fair that she herself had been helped by ice packs and medication. For some, it just takes time to work through those feelings and realize that all pain, all loss, is significant. For others, a grief therapist might be helpful to sort through and come to this understanding. If you think you would benefit by talking to a therapist, please consult with your doctor.

Take care of you

Continue to take care of yourself. Rest as much as you need to, and don't feel guilty about it. It may be a LONG time before you get your energy back.

If you are struggling with your emotional and/or mental well-being post-surgery, reach out to your doctor. There may also be a breast cancer support group in your area. It is a tremendous help to talk freely with others who truly understand what you have been through. Your local support group may have the option to meet in person or virtually. Check with your local American Cancer Society.

Helping others

Use your experience to reach out to others. Don't let your experience be for nothing. As the saying goes, "Never waste a good crisis." You are the only one who can tell your story.

You are probably thinking, "Who am I? Who would be interested in what I have to say, and what would I even tell them? How can I help anyone else?" Trust me when I say, I had those exact feelings. I want you to know that people are interested in what you have to say, you *can* help others, and your experience is extremely valuable! Put it in God's hands and allow Him to reach others through you.

When we rely on God, we are able to do great things – bigger than we can ever imagine – not because of us or who we are, but because of who God is. He is in control. I'm reminded of the story of Gideon in Judges 6. Gideon was beating out wheat in the winepress to hide it from the Midianites. An angel of the Lord appeared and told Gideon, "The Lord is with you, O mighty man of valor" (vs 13). There is irony here because Gideon was hiding, but the angel referred to him as a man of valor; valor means 'great courage in the face of danger.'

The angel tells him that he is to save Israel from the Midianites. Gideon's response was not one of bravery (think David facing Goliath). Instead, he replied,

> *"Please, Lord, how can I save Israel? Behold my clan is the weakest in Manasseh, and I am the least in my father's house." And the Lord said, "But I will be with you."* (ESV)

Gideon was anxious about what he was being called to do, so he asked God for a sign that it was truly Him speaking to him. He asked for a sign several times, actually. And God reassured Gideon each time. It turned out that God gave Gideon the weapons he needed (a torch, a clay jar, and a horn – not your normal weapons) and told Gideon where to position his army of 300 men. As ridiculous as it seems to do what God asks us to do – Gideon was called to lead his small army of men to defeat the Midianites, an army of 135,000 men, with only fire, a pot, and a horn – we must do our part before HE can do His part.

We cannot defeat an army with fire, a pot, and a horn, but God can. God can do great things through your story. Allow God to use you, just as Ms. Med allowed God to work through her, sharing her wisdom and experience to give me guidance.

Your story

Consider writing your own book. Your story is important, too. If for no one else, your family would appreciate hearing about your journey through your words, giving give them a deeper connection with you and your experience. Heather, one of my sisterhood friends, lost her mother when we were in our early thirties. She told me she would give anything to have her mom's story, in her own words, to pass along to her children. It will become something your family will treasure.

Husbands, love your wives as Christ loved the church and gave himself up for her

Ephesians 5:25 ESV

CHAPTER 5

RANDALL'S THOUGHTS – OBSERVATIONS FROM THE HUSBAND OF A CANCER SURVIVOR

"Play the hand you are dealt." No doubt you have heard this phrase throughout your life. In my experience it is almost always used as a response to something negative in someone's life that is also outside of that person's control. Maybe someone was born into a very poor home, maybe someone was raised by abusive parents, maybe someone lost a parent at an early age, maybe someone lost their job, or maybe someone's house burned down. In most card games, you have no control over what cards the dealer puts in your hand; similarly in life, there are certain conditions that you have no control over.

"Play the hand you are dealt" is also a lesson. Each of us learns that there will always be certain things in life that we have no control over, but despite this, we have to press on, adapt, and adjust in order to get on with life the best way possible.

The lesson of playing the hand you have been dealt was brought home to my family in a way I never imagined. Having read this far, you know that in 2018 my wife, Wendi, was diagnosed with breast cancer. Many of you know the feeling of getting bad news from your doctor. My wife and I were numb. We felt the shock, the uncertainty, and the fear of the unknown. Shortly after her diagnosis, we knew very little. Just how bad was it? Was her life in danger? Like a lot of people, my mind tends to go straight to the worst-case scenarios of what might happen. Suffice it to say, we were dealt a bad hand...now what?

"Now what?" indeed. Simple things, like knowing what to do next, were so difficult at that point in time. For example, we struggled with how to tell the kids, how to tell her parents, how to tell our friends, how to tell her coworkers and my coworkers. Simply the idea of what to do next was one of the toughest questions. Overcoming the inertia of the shock and being able to function well enough to make informed decisions was one of the main challenges.

The phrase "play the hand you are dealt" has two parts. The second part, "dealt," is really the first – you are dealt a hand. However, just because you know you have been dealt a bad hand does not mean you necessarily know all the details of what exactly you have been dealt. The first part, "play the hand," is the response to what you have been dealt and is the real lesson, and the real power, of the phrase. This is what my wife and I set out to do. We moved quickly to set up appointments (you never get medical answers as quickly as you would like to), and to figure out how to proceed.

This is when things took a turn. My wife and I had several discussions about how to find a good doctor. Let's face it, you rarely look for doctors before you have a reason. We had no idea which doctor we should see. My wife prayed to God for clarity. Soon those prayers were answered. One of the matriarchs at our church insisted on a meeting with my wife. It turned out that she had beaten breast cancer (something we had not been aware of), and practically insisted we use the same doctors she had used.

She told us about her procedures, the skill of her doctors, and the success of her treatment. We also soon found out that several other women we knew used the same doctors and clinic. The clarity my wife prayed for had been provided. So, we made an appointment at the Vanderbilt Breast Clinic in Nashville.

Over the next few months, we had several appointments with a team of doctors and nurses. During this time I had to alter my work schedule, often relying on my fellow staff to pick up what I couldn't carry. Also, as I traveled the state in the regular course of work, a number of people became aware of my wife's disease. Many offered their prayers and soon I was able to tell my wife that people, most total strangers to her, were praying for her from one end of Kentucky to the other.

The staff at Kentucky Rural Water Association, where I've worked for years, were a constant source of support for

Wendi and me, praying for us and helping me whenever necessary. Our church family was praying for us and offering help and food. And of course, my family and hers helped us, prayed for us, and cried with us.

Gradually I realized something that should have been obvious from Day One. Sure, my wife was dealt the bad hand of cancer, and we had to play that hand. However, in life we aren't just dealt one hand – we are dealt many hands and, unlike the common use of the phrase, we frequently have been dealt good hands as well.

We were dealt the good hand of having great friends who would do anything to help us. We were dealt the good hand of knowing people who had been through what we were going through (and worse) who were able to give us solid advice. We were dealt the good hand of having a skilled medical team. We were dealt the good hand of having wonderful work families, a wonderful church family, our own wonderful family, and a strong faith in God. We played those hands, over and over.

Looking back, the phrase "play the hand you have been dealt" offers several lessons that have become clear. First, play it. Play. The. Hand. That means you. No one else can play the hand for you. Remember, the bad hand is unavoidable and out of your control (at least initially). Running from the challenge, pretending it does not exist, will not help you. Wendi's cancer required our full attention and required planning. It forced us to rearrange our lives, to educate ourselves, to reach out to others, and to act in a timely fashion.

Second, play all of your hands. Use every good hand you hold. This requires you to have some self-awareness and for you to look outward, which can be difficult when you are going through one of the toughest challenges you have ever faced. To use another phrase, count your blessings. But don't just count the blessings – examine them, use them.

There are people in your life who can help, who want to help. Let them. Be willing to ask for and accept help. The wisdom of your elders and of people who have been through similar situations can be vital to your ability to deal with a problem. You don't have to figure everything out yourself, because others may already have the answers. Look for the wisdom of others.

The third lesson may be the most important. Life on Earth is imperfect. There is pain and there is sorrow. God does not promise us an easy life. God asks us to do unto others as we would have them do unto us. You are not the only person facing serious challenges in life – few people truly have it easy. In recognizing the good hands you have been dealt in life, the truly humbling revelation is that you are called to be the good hand dealt in other people's lives.

We are all called to be the good hand in other people's lives. This is true, maybe truer, if you have had to face some serious challenges yourself. You never know when that opportunity will come, and you may not even realize it when it happens, but it may be exactly what someone needs, exactly when they need it.

For whatever was written in former days was written for our instruction, that through endurance and through the encouragement of the scriptures, we might have hope.

Romans 15:4 ESV

CHAPTER 6

SCRIPTURES THAT HELPED ME

I turned to the Bible to find comfort during this time of uncertainty. There are so many scriptures that talk about God caring for us, watching over us, and letting us know He is with us; we are not alone. I wanted to share with you some of the scriptures that helped me most. I would read these over and over and over again. I suggest writing them out in your journal, on a sticky-note, or anywhere you can easily see them.

Maybe even put them on your bathroom mirror so you can see them every morning.

Psalm 46:10a ESV – "Be still, and know that I am God."

Isaiah 26:3-4 NCV – "You, Lord, give true peace to those who depend on You, because they trust You. So, trust the Lord always, because He is our Rock forever."

Lamentations 3:21-24 NIV – "Yet this I call to mind and therefore I have hope: Because of the Lord's great love, we are not consumed, for His compassions never fail. They are new every morning; great is Your faithfulness. I say to myself 'the Lord is my portion; therefore I will wait for Him.'"

Philippians 4:6-7 NLT – "Don't worry about anything; instead, pray about everything. Tell God what you need, and thank Him for all He has done. Then you will experience God's peace, which exceeds anything we can understand. His peace will guard your hearts and minds as you live in Christ Jesus."

Philippians 4:13 NLT – "For I can do everything through Christ, who gives me strength." (You are stronger than you think!)

Jeremiah 29:11 ESV – "For I know the plans I have for you, declares the Lord, plans for welfare and not for evil, to give you a future and a hope."

Deuteronomy 31:6 ESV – "Be strong and courageous. Do not fear or be in dread of them, for it is the Lord your God who goes with you. He will not leave you or forsake you."

Colossians 3:15a NLT – "And let the peace that comes from Christ rule in your hearts."

Deuteronomy 31:8 ESV – "It is the Lord who goes before you. He will be with you; He will not leave you or forsake you. Do not fear or be dismayed."

John 16:33 NIV – "I have told you these things, so that in me you may have peace. In this world you will have trouble. But take heart! I have overcome the world."

Psalm 18:29 ESV – "For by you I can run against a troop, and by my God I can leap over a wall."

Nahum 1:7 NASB – "The Lord is good, A stronghold in the day of trouble, And He knows those who take refuge in Him."

Jeremiah 17:7-8 NIV – "But blessed is the one who trusts in the Lord, whose confidence is in him. They will be like a tree planted by the water that sends out its roots by the stream. It does not fear when heat comes; its leaves are always green. It has no worries in a year of drought, and never fails to bear fruit."

Joshua 1:9 NIV – "Have I not commanded you? Be strong and courageous. Do not be afraid; do not be discouraged, for the Lord your God will be with you wherever you go."

Psalm 145:18 NIV – "The Lord is near all who call on him, to all who call on him in truth."

2 Corinthians 12:10 ESV – "For the sake of Christ, then, I am content with weakness, insults, hardships, persecutions, and calamities. For when I am weak, then I am strong."

I also took comfort in several songs and musical artists. In addition to Mandisa, Lauren Daigle was becoming well-known and I listened to her songs quite a bit, especially "Rescue" and "Trust in You." Another special song was by the band Casting Crowns. Some of the words are:

God of All My Days
Each step I take
You make a way
I will give You all my praise
My seasons change, You stay the same
You're the God of all my days
In my worry
God, you are my stillness
In my searching
God, you are my answers
In my blindness
God, you are my vision
In my bondage
God, you are my freedom
And in my weakness
God, you are my power
You're the reason that I sing
'Cause You are the God of all my days.[5]

Here is a space for you to write scriptures or songs that mean something to you:

_____
_____
_____
_____
_____
_____
_____
_____
_____
_____
_____
_____
_____
_____
_____
_____
_____
_____
_____
_____
_____
_____
_____
_____
_____
_____
_____
_____
_____
_____
_____
_____
_____

Let the words of my mouth
and the mediation of my heart
be acceptable in your sight,

O Lord,

my rock & my redeemer.

Psalm 19:14 ESV

CHAPTER 7

MY PRAYER FOR YOU

Prayer is such a wonderful gift from God. It gives us access to Him anytime – day or night – that we feel the need to call on Him. He is always available to us. ALWAYS. And I love that so much! I would like to pray for you now, if I may?

Holy and Divine Father,

You are Creator of our universe. You are awesome and all-powerful. We bow humbly in Your presence and before Your throne. We come together as one in Your Spirit. As we live in this world and experience its ups and downs, we are mindful that You are still the God who holds this whole world in Your hands. And Father, even in the ups and downs that life brings, we find great comfort in knowing we still sit in the palm of Your hand. We thank you for watching over us. For caring for us. For loving us. You have blessed us so richly, Father. All we have is because of You.

I come to You on behalf of all of those who are dealing with breast cancer, and all that goes with it. Father, You, more than anyone, know their struggles, both public and private. You know the impact this horrible disease has had on their physical, mental, emotional, and spiritual beings. But You were not surprised by any of this. You were not surprised by the diagnosis. You were there before the cancer started, when the cancer developed, and when the diagnosis was given.

And You will continue to be with them throughout the treatment process. I lift these cancer patients up to You, the Great Physician. If it is Your will, I ask for complete healing. Matthew 7:7 says that if we ask, it will be given to us. So, dear Lord, we are asking for healing. I pray for the entire scope of their needs – not only their physical needs, but their mental, emotional, and spiritual needs as well. Father, I ask that you hear my prayer.

I pray that those suffering reach out to You for comfort and guidance. May their hearts be full of peace over the situation. I pray they feel Your presence in an undeniable way and they experience You carrying them through this difficult time, because we know You are there. Please cover them with Your protection.

I pray that all breast cancer patients have a medical team that they are confident will provide the best care and treatment possible. It means so much to have trust and faith in those caring for us during such a scary time. Father, please guide the doctors, nurses, and surgeons who are caring for them. May they use their knowledge and wisdom to the patient's advantage. I ask that You guide the surgeon's hands during surgery and that nothing unexpected is found. I ask that you hear my prayer.

Heavenly Father, I ask that you watch over them during recovery. I pray they are able to rest and allow their body to heal. I had an easy recovery, Lord, with no complications, and I ask that they have the same experience. I pray their medication and treatments are beneficial to their prognosis and that the side effects are minimal. So many people suffer with the treatments more than the cancer itself, and they are miserable. I pray You watch over them and provide relief, if it is Your will.

Lord, I ask that You watch over their spouses and their children. They are also participating in this story, but they are watching things unfold from the sidelines. Sometimes, that is such a difficult place to be. Their immediate families have a front row seat to watch their loved one go through so much, and it can be heartbreaking.

The family wants to take away their pain, fatigue, nausea, and other stresses. They just want their loved one to feel better, and there is little they can do about the patient's physical aches. But Lord, the family can love and support them. The family can encourage them and just be available. I pray that the family members are able to show the patient how much they are loved and cared for, and that they feel this affection in a comforting way.

Father, I also want to ask that you be with their other family members and friends. They love them too, Lord, and they want to be there for them. When we have someone we care for going through a difficult time, we want to help them but are usually unsure how to do that. I pray that family and friends are able to support the patient with meals, cards, texts, phone calls, gifts, or anything else that would make them feel special. I pray that opportunities to serve them present themselves and that their loved ones act without hesitation.

Lord, I now pray for this book. My hope is that anyone reading this finds it helpful and it provides a bit of comfort, peace, and reassurance. I also pray, Father, that the reader can feel You through the words on the pages. Dear Lord, please forgive me for my stubbornness about writing this book. I waited so long to follow through what You placed on my heart years ago. I understand that *we* are Your hands, Your feet, and are here to share Your love with others. I have missed so many opportunities to do that, Father, and I am truly sorry. There may be others who are being called to act on Your behalf and are hesitating, for whatever reason. I pray that they find the courage to trust in You and move forward so they don't miss chances to share with others who You are.

Lord, please help us to listen more clearly for Your voice. The whisper. I know if we seek You first in all we do, You will not mislead us. Help us with discernment so that we know it is You and not our own voice we hear. I pray for all of us to work on our relationship with You so Your voice becomes more familiar to us. Father, hear our prayers.

We know that even in death, Lord, we have victory in Jesus. We are all spiritual beings having an earthly experience. We look forward to the time, if we have lived a life that You require of us, to being reunited with You and all of our loved ones who have gone on before us.

We love you, Father, and we praise You for all that You are. All the glory to You, the Almighty God. In Jesus Christ's majestic and holy name we pray, AMEN!

Here are some lined pages for you to write out your own prayers.

I will instruct you and teach you
in the way you should go;
I will counsel you with my
eye upon you.

Psalm 32:8 ESV

CHAPTER 8

THE EVIDENCE OF GOD'S WHISPERING

The writing of this book has been a story in itself. If I'm being perfectly honest, I am not a writer. I'm not really much of a 'reader' either. I can't sit still long enough and my attention span is that of a gnat, so reading has never been something I turn to for enjoyment and relaxation. However. God has been thumping me for three years now, and I have been coming up with one excuse after another for why I shouldn't write a book.

The main reason I gave Him for not putting my thoughts and experiences on paper was a question: "Who am I? I am no one important. What do I have to say that others would find valuable?" But God wouldn't let it be. He had been relentless.

It finally occurred to me that I am a daughter of the Living God and He wants me to tell my story. It isn't that I have something to say, because it isn't about me. However, God has plenty to say and He chose me to help get the word out.

This project has been a real struggle because it is way out of my comfort zone. God knows that. But how else can we grow, or bless someone else, if we don't challenge ourselves and follow through when He calls us to do something on His behalf?

My story actually started years before I learned of my breast cancer. Six of my girlfriends and I were in Gulf Shores, Alabama about 9 years prior to my diagnosis. We were standing on the boardwalk waiting to get into the famous Original Oyster House for supper, and we were hanging out, talking with each other. I remember exactly where we were standing. Cindy, one of my friends, made the comment that she recently got a Breast Cancer Awareness license plate because she wanted to support their cause. She then said, "Studies show that one in 7 women will get breast cancer, so that means one of us is likely to get it."

As soon as she said that, I heard a small voice in my head say, "It's going to be me." Then I thought, "What was that and where did that come from?" I didn't say anything to the girls at the time, because I thought it was so bizarre. Years later, when I got my breast cancer diagnosis, I was not surprised, because I remember the conversation in Alabama. I knew then that God had prepared me for what was to come. It was during the process of diagnosis and treatment that the title of the book, *God (Still) Whispers*, came to me. The idea behind the title is that God is active and living today in our lives, just as he was during the time the Bible was being written. He showed me over and over that He was with me every step of the way. I had confirmation many times that the decisions we were making were the right ones for me and my health.

Three years went by from the time I had mastectomy surgery to when I actually began writing the book. During that time, sentiments would come to me, or I would think of a particular verse, and say to myself, "If I ever write the book, that should go in it." I wish I would have jotted some of them down!

About the time I was, once again, feeling like God was urging me to write this book, I was in our church's ladies bible class. The teacher, asked us, "Do you ever argue with God?" I felt like I sunk in my seat, because, my answer was YES. I was arguing with God about why I shouldn't take on this project. I felt like He was poking at me once more. I am putting dates by the next series of events because I think it is important to point out how consistently God was reaching out to me, but I kept pushing back.

June 25th

A few weeks later, a friend's stepfather passed away and I went to the funeral home to see her and her family with some other friends. As we were coming out of the main room, getting ready to leave, my friend's cousin, Christy Harpring, was sitting by herself next to the door. This is important to the story because Christy had recently successfully launched her first book. Even though the book she wrote was a different genre than I was interested in writing, she knew the process and had some "do's and don'ts" experience. As we approached her, I heard in my head, "Ask her about the book." I thought that was not the time nor the place to have that conversation, so I didn't ask her.

July 14th

It took me some time to get up the nerve to reach out to Christy because the thought that "I may actually do this" was terrifying to me. When we were able to talk, I told her I felt like God was leading me to write a book about my breast cancer story, but I didn't feel capable. I said to her, "I mean, who am I? What do I have to offer that anyone would want to listen to me and my story?"

Christy replied, "It's so funny you should say that. I had a friend who recently went through breast cancer and treatment and she was looking for something encouraging to read for breast cancer patients. She told me that there isn't anything out there." That was humbling for me. 'Okay,' I thought to myself. 'Maybe I can offer some encouragement to someone.'

Another thing Christy and I talked about is how difficult it would be to write out my story, because it is so *personal*. The thought of sharing so much made me feel exposed. Christy told me, "Once you get over feeling like you've just walked naked into a room full of people, it will be better, and you'll be able to write more freely." She was right. That's exactly how it felt, and it did get better.

Christy also gave me the names of a couple of authors she knew, one in Savannah and one local to me. Christy knew Tonya Matthews from high school, and she had written a couple of books that aligned more with what I had planned to write. 'I'll reach out to Tonya if I decide I'm really going to write this book.' I thought to myself.

August 1st
    I was scrolling through Facebook, looking at what people had posted about their families. I belong to several inspirational group pages and I was looking at their posts as well.
    Then I saw it. I saw what the cover of my book was going to look like. That is, if I decided to actually write the book. It was an antique white wooden cabinet that had two drawers and two doors. The drawers and doors were painted a beautiful green. The paint on the cabinet was distressed. The front had ornate carving down each side. Sitting on top of the cabinet was a white bucket with pink, white, and purple flowers and greenery. The photo spoke to me in a very loud way. I thought it was perfect.
    I then realized the picture had words at the bottom of the image. It said, "Never ignore a nudge or whisper from God." Woah. There was God, again, poking me.

August 12th
    I received a private message from Tonya Matthews on Facebook. She was getting ready to launch her second book and sent me an invite to a reception she was hosting at her home. I was surprised when I got her message out of the blue (as far as I was concerned, but God was not surprised). And there sat, right next to my laptop, the piece of paper where I had written Tonya's name during my conversation with Christy. I was supposed to reach out to her and I hadn't yet. But God used Tonya to move me along in the process of this project. The next day I messaged her back and told her that I had been meaning to contact her, and that I wanted her guidance on the book writing process.

August 16th

Tonya and I had a phone conversation and talked about several things. She gave me the rundown of her experience both in writing her books and in self-publishing. We also talked about other authors who were of the same genre as ours. One of the authors she mentioned was Laurie Cline, another local author who had just released a book. Tonya suggested I reach out to her and encouraged me to read her book. Laurie's book addresses her family's struggles, and how, with God's help, they were able to get through that difficult time in their lives.

August 19th

I had been home for several weeks recovering from a recent surgery and was in our sunroom messing around on my laptop. I was getting hungry and I felt like I had enough energy that I could fix spaghetti for supper. It was only Randall and me, after all. Nothing too fancy and it didn't require a lot of work.

I love listening to music and I like to have my radio on anytime I am in the kitchen, so I turned it on as I began preparing to cook supper. Instead of music playing as I expected, there was a podcast being broadcast. Literally, the first words I heard coming out of the speaker were, "It was almost as if the chapter wrote itself." Another God poke! I thought, "Okay…. Okay God. Let me get supper started and let's just see where this goes." While spaghetti was cooking, I sat back down at my laptop and I said out loud, "Okay, God. Let's do this. Let's see where this is going to go. What do You want me to say?" By the time supper was finished cooking, I had a one-page outline. Chapters were laid out. There in front of me were the bones of the book. I plugged in events and conversations where they belonged and, about nine pages later, I had the beginning of my book.

August 23rd

I received a private message from Laurie Cline. She heard from Tonya that I had recently purchased her book and that I was tossing around the idea of writing one myself. She told me she hoped her book blessed me and then offered her guidance and said I could use her as a resource, if needed. This was another God poke. Several people had been put in my path who could help me see this project through. It provided me a sense of confirmation that this was, indeed, what God wanted me to do. I was a bit stubborn, like Gideon. I kept thinking, 'God, if this is *really* what you want me to do, give me a sign.' He did, over and over.

I continued to write when I could. Each time I sat down, I would say, "God, what do You want me to say?" I would get inspiration at church, or talking with friends, and think, 'Oh, that needs to be added to the book.' It was a balance of "Hurry up and get it written" and "Be patient to make sure everything God wants included is there."

One of the reasons I was hesitant to write this book is because I would have to relive some details of the whole experience again. I wasn't excited about that prospect. October is somewhat of a difficult month for me. It is the month set aside to bring awareness to breast cancer and cancer research, and to celebrate breast cancer survivors. I appreciate the idea but sometimes I just want to forget I went through that experience. But I am truly grateful for the opportunity to help others.

It was important to me, and my story, to include the names of those I interacted with during this time. I wanted to make the point that, even the smallest conversation, action, or deed *does* matter and can have a lasting impact.

Everyone's walk is a little different. But I hope this book gives you a starting point that you can individualize as your story unfolds. God continues to show Himself to me on a regular basis. I pray that you are able to see Him active in your life, as well. May God bless us all.

Randall and me just before the 5K walk. It was so cold!

The 10K/5K team: Patti Pitcock, Crystal Folker, Wendi Kelley, Sydney Clingenpeel, Patrick Folker, Jeff Galloway, Randall Kelley, Stephanie Lindsey, Chris Lindsey, Melanie Clingenpeel, Chris Jernigan, and Emily Jernigan. Wearing our purple "Think Pink, Walk Proud" shirts.

#runliketheWendi

My Walk by Faith, I am an Overcomer, and #Sisterhood
bracelets that became my shield, of sorts. I felt God
protected me when I wore them.

APPENDIX A

Diagnosis

What type of cancer do I have?

_____

_____

_____

_____

Is it an aggressive type?

_____

_____

_____

_____

Where is the tumor located?

_____

_____

_____

_____

How big is the tumor?

_____

_____

_____

_____

What stage is the tumor?

_____

_____

_____

_____

Is the cancer in my lymph nodes?

_____

_____

_____

_____

What is my estrogen receptor (ER) and progesterone
receptor (PR) status?

_____

_____

_____

_____

What is my HER2 status?

_____

_____

_____

_____

Is a port recommended for treatment so repeated needle
sticks won't be necessary?

_____

_____

_____

_____

Should I be concerned with being immunocompromised? If
so, how will that be handled?

_____

_____

_____

_____

Surgery

If surgery is the best option, do you recommend a lumpectomy? Mastectomy?

_____

_____

_____

_____

Will any lymph nodes be removed during surgery?

_____

_____

_____

_____

How much clear margin is expected?

_____

_____

_____

_____

What types of bandages/drains will be used?

_____

_____

_____

_____

How invasive is the surgery?

_____

_____

_____

_____

Can anything be saved?

_____

_____

_____

_____

Is reconstruction surgery an option?

_____

_____

_____

_____

If so, when would it be done?

_____

_____

_____

_____

Implants

Are implants wanted/necessary?

_____

_____

_____

_____

Is it possible for both the surgeon and the plastic surgeon to work together during one surgery?

_____

_____

_____

_____

If I am having a single mastectomy, do you suggest getting an implant on the other side as well, for symmetry?

_____

_____

_____

_____

Does the plastic surgeon recommend saline or silicone implants?

_____

_____

_____

_____

Is there an expiration date on the implants?

_____

_____

_____

_____

Does the plastic surgeon have photos of other patients so their work can be seen?

_____

_____

_____

_____

Website:

_____

_____

_____

_____

If I lose or gain weight after the surgery, will it affect the look of the implants/breasts?

_____

_____

_____

_____

Treatment

What are the treatment options: Chemo? Radiation? An oral medication like Tamoxifen?

_____

_____

_____

_____

If I have been through menopause, does that make a difference in my treatment options?

_____

_____

_____

_____

If radiation is necessary, what is the preparation procedure?

_____

_____

_____

_____

How long will this process be before my first radiation treatment?

_____

_____

How will you know where to administer the radiation?

_____

_____

_____

_____

Recovery

What is the time period for treatment and medication?

_____

_____

_____

_____

If it is necessary to take time off from work, how long is recovery expected to take?

_____

_____

_____

_____

What restrictions will I have?

_____

_____

_____

_____

Will I have to adjust how I sleep?

_____

_____

_____

_____

Will I need to have physical therapy following surgery?

_____

_____

_____

_____

Space for additional questions.

_____

_____

_____

_____

_____

_____

_____

_____

_____

_____

_____

_____

_____

_____

_____

_____

_____

_____

_____

Some other goodie basket ideas are:

Have	Item	Have	Item
	Deodorant wipes		Travel-size tissue
	Flexible straws		Cleansing wipes
	Lip balm		Lotion
	Makeup remover wipes		Hat, scarf, and/or turban
	PJs with button-down top		Comfy tops with buttons
	Cardigan sweater		Fuzzy socks
	Fluffy robe		Small round ice packs
	Chest pillow		Small pillow for under arm
	Seatbelt pillow		Wedge pillow
	Blanket		Planner/calendar
	Magazines		Puzzle books/pens
	Thank You cards/stamps		Books
	Gift certificates/coupons		Restaurant gift cards
	Snacks and/or fruit		Bottles of juice or water
	Powerade or Gatorade		A journal
	Aquaphor Healing Ointment		Calendula Cream

NOTES

NOTES

ENDNOTES

[1] (2022, January 29). *Key Statistics for Breast Cancer in Men.* American Cancer Society. https://www.cancer.org/cancer/breast-cancer-in-men/about/key-statistics.html

[2] (2022, January 29). *U.S. Breast Cancer Statistics,* Breastcancer.org. https://www.breastcancer.org/symptoms/understand_bc/statistics

[3] 2022, February 16). *National Cancer Institute,* Cancer.gov. https://www.cancer.gov/publications/dictionaries/cancer-terms

[4] Dossey, Larry. (1994) *Healing Words: The Power of Prayer and the Practice of Medicine.* HarperCollins.

[5] Source: Musixmatch. Songwriters: Jason Ingram / John Mark Mark Hall. God of All My Days lyrics © My Refuge Music

ACKNOWLEDGEMENTS

First, I would like to thank Almighty God for all the blessings He has given. For the gift of salvation, for His unending love, and for always being available to me. I thank Him for walking with me during this project as this was written to honor Him. I pray it is able to reach people in a way that glorifies Him!

My husband, Randall Kelley, is my rock in the midst of storms. We've always said when chaos is swirling all around us, we are able to come together for peace and calm. You were an answer to a prayer long ago and I love you dearly.

My children, Cash (Amy) Wilson, Micah Medrano (Ryan), and Jack Kelley (Maria). My treasure on earth. I love you deeply and am so proud of you! Your prayers and unending love made such a difference in my healing process.

My grandkids, Sophie, Bronx, Rorie, Haddie, Carrigan, and Hailey. The lights of my life! I adore each one of you and you are so very special to me. Thank you for loving your Bibi so BIG!

My parents, Art and Kathy Harris. I owe so much of who I am to them and my up-bringing. They taught me about God and what family truly means. They have always been an outstanding example of people being able to trust you at your word and help others when you can. Their prayers, love, and support carried me through many trying times and I am forever grateful.

My brothers Alex (Frances) and Ricky Harris. They have been some of my biggest prayer warriors and cheerleaders of all! Frances loves me like a sister and I love her dearly, too.

My tribe: Amy Hubbard, Heather Hughes, Laurie McCombs, Cindy Stinnett, Michelle Tedder. I am extremely blessed to have had you all in my life for so many years. You all mean the world to me and I can't imagine doing this life without you! I cherish the memories we have already made, and can't wait to experiences those that are ahead of us. #Sisterhood

Patrick and Crystal Folker. I thank you for all the love, prayers, and support you've shown me. Patrick – I can't thank you enough for being willing to share your God-given talent and painting the images for the covers of the book. Crystal – Thank you for all the prayers and support, but especially for always being so willing to give me one of your famous hugs! Those hugs are so special!

Stephanie Lindsey and Sammie G. I appreciate you both more than I can put in to words. You were always there for me whenever I needed you. God certainly used you both to bless me, and I thank you for being willing to allow Him to use you.

Medrith and Lannas Anschultz. My sister and brother in Christ. My mentors. You both are so special to me. Ms. Med was willing to allow God to use her in an answer our prayers and provided the "guidance and clarity" that I needed. I am forever grateful.

Alvaton Church of Christ. My beloved church family. I can't thank you all enough for how you rallied around me and my family. Your love and prayers helped us through our "bump in the road". May God richly bless each one of you!

My coworkers at GFCB – Thank you for all of your support. I was able to focus on recovery and healing without having to worry about what was going on at the office. I am blessed to work with such a caring group.

To those mentioned throughout this book – many, many thanks to each of you for your role in my story. You all provided guidance, wisdom, compassion, and confirmation that the decisions we were making were the best for me and my situation. Thank you for allowing God to use you!

Vanderbilt Breast Center and my medical team – Ms. Carol, Dr. Grau, Dr. Abramson, and Dr. Higdon. I can't thank you enough for your wisdom, compassion, and tender care. I felt like I literally put my life in your hands and you gave me the best experience, under the circumstances, possible.

Christy Harpring, Tonya Matthews, Laurie Cline. Thank you all for sharing your wisdom of writing a book with me. You gave me guidance when I didn't even know where to begin.

Sedrik Newbern. A BIG thank you for all your guidance to actually get this book into print. I couldn't have done it without you!

Linda Wolf, my editor. You are THE BEST! You helped take my manuscript up a notch and I am grateful for your time and energy.

Leslie Jones. Your graphic design skill and talents took my vision to the next level. You are amazing!

Wendi Kelley is a first-time author. She is honored to share her breast cancer story in hopes that it encourages others going through the process to turn to God and listen to His whispers. She has been married to Randall for twenty-two years; they have three children, Cash (Amy), Micah (Ryan), and Jack (Maria). They have six grandchildren, Sophie, Bronx, Rorie, Haddie, Carrigan, and Hailey.

CAN YOU HELP?

Thank you from the bottom of my heart for taking the time to read my book! I really appreciate all of the feedback and comments. I love hearing what you have to say.

If you would be so kind as to leave me an honest review letting me know your opinion of the book, how it helped you, who you gifted it to, etc., I would be grateful.

May God be with us all,

Wendi Kelley

Made in the USA
Coppell, TX
12 April 2023